Momma's
A Preschool Owner

Loralee Lovell

ISBN: 1495489876
ISBN-13: 9781495489877

DEDICATION

This book is dedicated to my super supportive
hubby, Jens...for always letting me be the kite
while you are the string!
Also, to my 5 kiddos...
Brienne, Reagan, Cael, Carter, and Emmi!
You all keep me on my toes and allow me to create crazy ideas
and being there with me through them all!
Love every single one of you!

CONTENTS

Why did I decide to start a Preschool?

I would consider myself someone that has an

Entrepeneur Spirit. I love to have an outlet

for my creativity and I found that opening a

Preschool was the way to go about it! Being

a wife and the momma of 5 kiddos (3 of which are

preschool age), I found that this was a great

avenue to own my own business and include my

kiddo's in it!

Opening a Preschool is easier now then ever! Would you love to Own your own business?

Want to bring in some income?

Need to have an outlet for your creativity?

Keep on reading for my step by step guide!

Why did I choose Preschool over Daycare?

Like I said at the beginning...I am the momma of 5

kiddos! I don't have time to watch other people's

kiddos all hours of the day and night. The fact of

the matter is, you work less and get paid more.

Sound too good to be true? It isn't! This was an

obvious choice for myself and my family.

When you read this "book"...you will notice that all

chapters (I don't know if you can even call them

Chapters) are short & sweet! If you are like

me...my attention span is not all that long. So, I

have condensed everything so you don't have to be

yawning while reading! You're Welcome!

CHAPTER 1

SO.....WHERE DO YOU BEGIN?

You need to start with finding out what your state

requirements are. Some states do

not require a whole lot, others are very strict. In

my state, as long as you stay under 4

hours a day, you do not have to be state certified.

If you are in a very strict state, then

you just need to be a little more creative. But, I

promise, it is worth it. Just do a search

online to get your state's requirements before

beginning. Remember that you are

opening a preschool and **not** a daycare. They are

two different things. So, the

requirements are not the same, in most cases.

Chapter 2

CPR/FIRST AID is ALWAYS A GOOD IDEA

You may or may not be required to be certified,

but I feel that you should always be

CPR/FIRST AID certified. It's great to have even

without owning a preschool. You can

get certified at your local hospital, college or

university, community programs, etc. It

usually only takes a couple of hours and it is a

good idea to stay up on all the changes

that they have made to better help those in

trouble.

Chapter 3

Inspection Time!

What ever location you decide on, either your home, or a public place, you will need a inspection done on that space. You will need to contact your city to find out who is responsible to inspect space. Usually there will be someone from the fire department coming to make sure that there is safety there. They will instruct you on what you need to make it the safest place possible. Every city, county, and state have different requirements. Find out from your local city what those requirements are.

Chapter 4

Do You need a Degree?

Nope! Some parents will prefer that you have one,

and others don't even ask. As long as

you are a great preschool teacher...you are good

to go!

(See...like I said, can you even call this a chapter?)

Chapter 5

Insurance

It may or not be a requirement...but it is a good idea to have! Talk to a local or non-local Insurance agent and see what it covered! Just to be on the safe side!!

Now that we are done with the "nitty-gritty"...we are ready to move on to the Fun Stuff!

Chapter 6

Choosing your name & logo!

This is where my creative juices get flowing. If you don't care about having a "catchy" name, then you use your first or last name or both and come up with for example..."Elizabeth's Preschool". If you are wanting to be a little different and fun, then you need to brainstorm.

For me...I wanted the name of my preschool to be a brand! A logo and name that was catchy and cute and memorable. Something that if someone saw it on the back of my car or shirt, that I would get compliments and they would remember. That's exactly what happened.

Here are some ways to pick the perfect business name:

• Start by thinking of what you want your business name to communicate

• It should reinforce that you own a preschool

• The more your name communicates preschool, the less explaining you have to do

• Make sure that it is name that people can relate to and understand

• Don't pick a name that is too long or confusing

• Stay away from cute puns that only you understand

Very Important! Go online to register your business, and this is where you can see if the name is already taken, and if it's not, this is where you pay a small fee to register your business online. Then your business name is officially YOURS! Yay!

Once your business name is decided, start building the enthusiasm and get others excited about it. Your name is the first step towards your business identity.

When picking a logo, follow these points

- A logo must be SIMPLE

- A logo must be MEMORABLE

- A logo must be APPROPRIATE

- A logo must be VERSATILE

How do you find someone to do a logo?

- Find someone local

- Go to an online auction

- Talk to computer friend

Your business name and logo will be used for advertising on your car, in ads, banners, business cards, shirts, blog, and website. Make sure this is done before moving on.

Chapter 7

Location, Location, Location

Here are some ideas of where to do a preschool. There are so many options of places to house your preschool.

Preschool in Your Own Home

There are options if you are doing it in your own home. You can make your garage into a preschool. If you own a basement, you can turn the entire or partial basement into your preschool. Or you can use a space inside your house that you designate for the preschool.

Pros of Having a Preschool in Your Home

- The place of business is in your home.

- You don't have to leave your house to "go to work".

- You can write off some of the area in your taxes because you are using some of your house for your business.

- You don't have to have to pay "extra" rent for the space.

- You can prepare your school area without leaving

Cons of Having a Preschool in Your Home

• It's in your home. You can never really "leave" work.

• If your kids love to get into everything, like mine do...it's hard to keep them out of Preschool things

• You lose space in your home

Commercial Property

You can always rent a commercial space.

Depending on where you live, there can be lots

i

of commercial properties available.

Pros of Commercial Property

• Some may feel it is a more "legit" business

• You usually have the options of having signage, which equals advertising

• You may be surrounded by other businesses, which again, is advertising for you

• You can keep business there without bringing it home

• The space may be bigger than something your own home can offer

Cons of Commercial Property

- You have to sign a lease

- You will have the extra expense of a down payment. You can always ask to stretch the deposit out over time.

- They may want a business plan

- They may check your credit

- You have to drive to "work", added gas expense

- You may be around other businesses that bother you

Adding your Preschool into Current Locations

There are a lot of dance studios, gymnastic gyms, karate places that would love to rent you a space in their location. They may already have a separate room, or you may need to build a wall, etc. These studios feel like it would be helpful to them as well.

If you are bringing in more kids into their location, the possibility exists that they will get some new customers from you and the same works in your favor as well.

If the parents know that there is a preschool in the same location that they know and trust, it's a good way to bring in customers as well. *I even had my preschool in the back of a Children's Boutique

i

Store. Parents shopped while kids were in school.

Pros of Sharing a Location

• Costs are a lot lower than renting out an entire commercial space

• Free advertising

• Possibility of adding dance, gym, etc to their preschool experience

• The building usually will already have been inspected, so you won't have to do that

Cons of Sharing a Location

- You are sharing a location with someone

- You may or may not get along with the other business owner

- You may have to add a wall to separate the area

- It may be busy and distracting while doing preschool

Chapter 8

Location....Check! Now What?

Now, is the fun part of setting up your location!
There are so many pictures online and on
Pinterest (especially) that will give you all sorts of
ideas!

Pick colors you want to see in your preschool (here's a little color psychology for ya)

• **Blue** has been considered a favorite color in many studies. Blue has been shown to slow pulse rate & lower body temp. A soothing color.

- **Green** is another favorite. It's a little more versatile. It is a soothing color and also represents vigor, youth, and renewal.

- **Red**. Not a great wall color for preschool. It's all about energy & excitement. It actually raises blood pressure and makes the heart beat faster.

- **Pink** is a very soft and calming color (even though it's a light tint of red)

- **Yellow** is a great interior color. Just like sunshine, it shows happiness, hope, and optimism. Studies have shown that the brain actually releases more seratonin when the eye takes in yellow. This can stir up creative juices.

- **Orange** is a happy color as well. Orange has a warmth and energy about it. But, if you are looking for calm, this may not the color to use.

- **Purple** is a tricky color. Adding this for splashes of color would be best!

- **Black** is great for accents in the room, too much can be depressing.

- **White** is peaceful and will make a room appear larger than it is.

Remember that your preschool needs to be an inviting place. This is where your little students will be spending a couple of hours each day. They need to feel comfortable there.

I cannot stress enough that having little people sized tables, chairs, couches, etc is important. This will allow them to feel "big". This will also help with injuries. There will be less falling off then if they were on big people things. They also feel so independent if they can sit down at their chair without any help.

There are so many options on what to add to your classroom. Here are some ideas:

- Little couches in a reading area

- tables and chairs for writing, eating snack, coloring, art

- Large rug (for circle time) this is where everyone can gather for a lesson, singing time, the flag salute, etc

- Picnic Tables, for snack time, if you have enough room (just little ones)

- Centers (dividing areas of the classroom for different subjects)

- Paint a chalkboard wall (just use a small can of chalkboard paint)

- Put up flannel boards on the wall

- Make a magnetic board on the wall

- Use bathroom backsplash material for a dry-erase board (sounds weird but it's the same stuff, and a whole heck of a lot cheaper)

- Cubby's for shoes and papers (label with their name...this helps with routine)

- Coat hangers (label with their name...this helps with routine)

- Vinyl lettering (I had a super cute tree made out of letters...it was a hit!)

Again, look online for wonderful ideas. Things will change around once you have students, and you can get a better feel for what is needed with your specific kiddos. I promise!

**Important....make sure your new location has been inspected and passed!

Chapter 9

Numbers

Now is the time to decide on what days, hours, ages of kids, the amount of kids, curriculum, and price you will be charging. So once again, let's break this down.

• **Days.** I have tried several things and it is whatever works best for you and your family that school year.

You can choose to do all 5 days for 1 class. You can divide the days up like Monday,

Wednesday, Friday. You can do Tuesday and Thursday. My latest was Tuesday, Wednesday, and Thursday, which allowed me to get fully prepared on Monday and have a 3 day weekend to recover.

- **Hours**. Again, I have tried it all. One thing though....In most states, if you want to own a preschool without having to be state certified, you have to keep the hours lower. So, here it is 4 hours a day.

With that said, I have done 2 hours in the am and 2 hours in the afternoon. I have done just morning classes for 2-3 hours as well. It is up to you if you have the time to do morning and afternoon. Just make sure that you know your state laws when it comes to the amount of hours per day with or without being state certified.

- **Amount of Kiddos.** There could be a maximum according to state laws, so check that out. Depending on the group of kids you have that sign up, you may want to divide up the age groups.

I have had years where I do ages 2-3 on Tues and Thursday and then the older kids ages from 4-5 will be on Monday, Wednesday, and Fridays, which allows more time to prepare for kindergarten. I have also done all ages together and we divide the ages up during class with my teacher's aid(s). So again, it all depends on what you want.

- **Curriculum.** You can either come up with your own by looking online, or you can order pre-done curriculum (which I will be offering soon), or you can purchase books with the ideas already there. Again, there is a lot of information out there!

- **How much to Charge.** This is where it gets a little bit tricky. Every city and state has such a difference in how much people are willing to pay.

  Check around what is being charged in your

local area and come up with a price that will cover all your costs and put some money in your pocket, since this is why you are owning a business.

You need to be honest with yourself! DO NOT short yourself and charge too low. It will become very tiresome if you don't see the financial reward every month.

I charge a one-time registration fee and then a set fee every month due on the first school day of every month. "Normally", you should get at least$200 to $4,000+ a month, depending on amount of kids and where you live.

**Important....with Money comes Taxes. Make sure that you are setting aside money for taxes. Having an accountant would be super helpful!

Chapter 10

Now Time To Advertise!

This is where you get all your clients! But guess what?! Advertising Does NOT have to cost you an arm or leg! Here's how:

- **Social Media!** This is huge! There are a lot of people using social media now...you will be able to get to a lot of people this way. Set your own page and use instead of a website or a blog or have it along with them.

- **Pediatricians/Dental.** Ask to put up your business cards at their office. Usually there is not a problem

- **Children's Boutiques/Consignment Stores.** Again, see if you can put your cards or brochures there.

- **Dance Studios/Gyms/Karate, etc**. Go where the kids are!

- **On your Car!** Get your logo put on your car! Cheap & Simple Vinyl works great! Have your contact info on there, including your website and/or blog. You will be amazed what interest you can get from that. I have even received calls from people that are calling me from another state while we were visiting. So, I know it works. Plus, your car can be a tax write-off!

- **Children's Events.** Once again, bring your cards, brochures, etc

- **Pay Money for Newspaper Advertisements**. I personally have never used this option. I just don't think that a ton of people are reading the paper anymore.

- **Pay money for Phone Book Listing.** Again, I don't think a ton of people are looking in phone books anymore. But, remember that every location is different.

- **WORD OF MOUTH!!** As you get going with preschool...and if it's a great experience....then I promise you....people will share your name! It has been my greatest way of getting new preschoolers. This is HUGE!

You now have a preschool!

- Have an open house

- Set up your preschool rules & share it with your parents

- Send out newsletters weekly or monthly

- Offer Field trips (make sure parents are driving their own kid for liability purposes)

- Make sure hat you have a contract of liability signed by each parent. Very

Important. Check out online to see the many

different types of forms that you should/can have

to protect yourself and your family.

• Be yourself! Have Fun!

• If you have any questions and/or want to be a part of my
monthly tips & tricks for Preschool Owners...please email
me at loraleelovell@gmail.com

If you follow the steps I have outlined for you...it will make
it a lot easier than if you were trying to go blindly into this!
Take it from my experience!Here's to your future

...as a Preschool Business Owner!

Congrats!!!